BEAUTIFUL BEASTIES

BEAUTIFUL BEASTIES

text by Mike Ashley

illustrations by David Mostyn

Robinson Children's Books

First published in the UK by Robinson Children's Books,
an imprint of Constable & Robinson Ltd, 2001

Constable & Robinson Ltd
3 The Lanchesters
162 Fulham Palace Road
London W6 9ER
www.constablerobinson.com

Text © Mike Ashley
Illustrations © David Mostyn 2001
Typeset and coloured by Oxford Designers & Illustrators
Edited by Sue Nicholson

NESTLÉ and SMARTIES are registered trademarks of
Société des Produits Nestlé S.A., 1800 Vevey, Switzerland.
© 2001 Société des Produits Nestlé S.A., 1800 Vevey, Switzerland.
Trade Mark Owners.

All rights reserved. This book is sold subject to the condition
that it shall not, by way of trade or otherwise, be lent, resold,
hired out or otherwise circulated in any form of binding or
cover other than that in which it is published and without a
similar condition being imposed on the subsequent purchaser.

A copy of the British Library Cataloguing in Publication Data
for this title is available from the British Library.

ISBN 1 84119 407 7

10 9 8 7 6 5 4 3 2 1

Contents

What is a beastie anyway? — 6–7

Hot-blooded beasties — 8–31
From lions and tigers to giant pigs and
mighty mammoths, this section covers
lots of the world's big land beasties.

Cold-blooded beasties — 32–47
Here are some of the world's most
dangerous and vicious creatures –
including the biggest man-eater ever!

Beasties of the deep — 48–65
Some of the weirdest, strangest, biggest
and ugliest beasties of all time.

Flap-mungus beasties — 66–77
Not all birds are fluffy, cute and cuddly.
Here are some flap-mungus beasties of
the air.

Creepy-crawly beasties — 78–95
Beetles, spiders, snakes, worms and all
kinds of slithery, scuttling and hairy
minibeasties.

Index — 96

WHAT IS A BEASTIE ANYWAY?

When you hear someone say the word 'beastie', what do you think they mean? Usually they mean something unpleasant, frightening and totally disgusting. And sometimes dangerous!

But beasties can also be beautiful. We can wonder at these fantastic creatures. The blue whale, elephant, sharks, snakes, giant spiders are all amazing creatures and truly something to marvel at.

And that's what this book is all about. To look at the incredible world of beautiful beasties.

Inside you'll find beasties that are huge and disgusting and horrible and creepy and frightening and nasty. But they are also beautiful and amazing and unbelievable and fantastic.

So don't be afraid. Have fun!

Mike Ashley.

HOT-BLOODED BEASTIES

Did you know that a gorilla can lift heavier weights than an elephant but that a hyena is more vicious than either of them? Or that a puma can leap 7m straight into the air from a standing start?

This part of the book covers the world's biggest and hairiest and fastest and fattest land mammals. You'll meet

- cats that can swim faster than an Olympic athlete
- hippo-mungus piles of poo
- monster pigs
- the eeriest howl in the world
- bears as big as cars
- apes that need ear-muffs
- belly-button-licking tongues
- more rats than you can count
… and a lot more.

So just turn the page for some monstermammaltastic facts.

Monster moggy

There are all sorts of big cats – and by that I mean cats a lot bigger than your pet cat. The biggest cat in the world is the Siberian tiger. It can grow up to 2.8m in body length plus another 1m of tail, and it weighs around 300kg. That makes it 66 times heavier than a pet cat!

GET THIS!

A tiger is immensely strong. It can drag prey so heavy that it would take a dozen men to move it. And that's even over walls. So it could easily drag you and your school bag over the school gates …

A big bite

The tiger is the only big cat known to eat humans. A tiger can crush a human skull with just one bite of its jaws (so one could soon gobble you up for breakfast). One notorious tiger was supposed to have killed and eaten over 500 people during the six years from 1959 to 1965.

A lion is almost as big as a tiger. It can grow up to 2.8m long and weigh 250kg. A lioness can run faster than a tiger – up to 80km/h in a short burst of speed. It's always the lioness that does all the hunting. Mr Lion lies there and supervises (but he does roar a lot).

CAT OLYMPICS

Big cats are famous for their speed and agility. But which do you think would win each event in a cat Olympics?

Track and Field

The 100 metres – the cheetah, in 3.6 seconds
The cheetah is the fastest of the monster cats. It can reach a maximum speed of 100km/h in just three seconds. These cats are lithe and light. A cheetah weighs only about 55kg – that's probably about the same as a full-grown Great Dane.

The 200 metres – the cheetah, in 7.2 seconds
A cheetah can keep up its speed for about 20 seconds and can cover a lot of ground in that time, but it soon starts to tire.

The 400 metres – the lion, in 18 seconds
Even though they can run fast, both a lion and a tiger would lose out to an antelope, which can run 800m at a constant 88km/h – handy if you're on a lion's lunch menu.

The high jump – the puma, 7m
The puma or mountain lion is the best jumper in the cat world. One puma was seen to leap 7m straight up from standstill. That would be like you jumping on to the roof of a house. Another puma leapt almost 12m in a single bound.

The long jump – the snow leopard, 15m
That would be like you leaping across a tennis court – that's nearly the length of five cars laid end to end.

Swimming

The 50 metre dash – the tiger and jaguar (dead heat)
This would be a tight one between the tiger and the jaguar. The jaguar is the cat world's best swimmer and has been known to steal people off small boats during the night. The tiger can swim up to 29km/h – that's nine times faster than the Olympic record holder! A tiger can swim 50m in 6.2 seconds!

11

Super-dogs

Although all dogs are descended from the wolf, the wolf isn't the biggest or the fastest. Check out these monster muts.

- The heaviest dog is the St Bernard, which can weigh up to 134kg – over half as heavy again as the wolf.
- The tallest dog is the Great Dane, which can reach 1m tall when standing on all fours, making it a head taller than a wolf.
- The fastest dog is the greyhound, which can belt along at a whopping 67km/h.

But in a head-to-head fight, a wolf would almost certainly defeat all three of these dogs, and more!

Super-friends

Is your best friend a dog?

GET THIS!

In 1978, 5-year-old Kenny Homme fell into a creek which was flooded because of heavy rain. The water carried Kenny into a tunnel, where he would certainly have drowned, but at that point, the family dog, Chester, who had struggled through raging water for 10 minutes, reached Kenny. The boy was able to climb onto the dog's back and Chester brought him back to safety.

A dog's life

Wolves are the ancestors of all dogs. They hunt in packs and are amongst the most efficient of hunters. A wolf pack will almost always get its prey. A pack of wolves can chase down and kill an animal as big as a moose.

GET THIS!

The eerie howl of a Canadian timber wolf can give you the shivers. But it's not meant to be scary – it's a warning. Wolves have a superb sense of smell and of hearing and can often detect forest fires before other animals. A wolf's howls echo through the forest and can be heard by other wolves for over 130 sq km.

Another pack hunter

Which animal looks like a dog, is more closely related to a cat but whose name means 'pig-like'?
Answer: a hyena!

Hyenas start fighting each other from the day they are born. Brother fights brother, sister fights sister, males taunt females, and the mother hyena is the angriest of the lot. When they're tired of fighting each other they'll take on anything else, including a lion.

Hyenas are vicious killers. Once they've clamped their teeth into an animal, they will not let go, no matter what happens. A pack of hyenas has been known to kill and eat a gnu in just 15 minutes.

Hyenas grow quite big. Adults can grow up to 90cm tall and 2m long and weigh 80kg. They can run at speeds of more than 60km/h.

Krazy kanga

Did you know that kangaroos can't walk backwards? And they'd have a real problem with a revolving door.

Kangaroos can go for months without drinking water. In order to keep cool, they dribble over themselves. When they do need water, they dig a well, often as much as 1.2m deep.

Monster leapers

The giant red kangaroo is about the same height as a human but is much faster. It bounds along at 64km/h and can leap 13m in one go. That's half as far again as the greatest jump ever made by a man, equal to about the length of three cars.

A kangaroo can bound as high as 3.2m, so one could easily jump right over a garden shed!

Kangaroos are bigger than you might think, standing 1.8m high with a 1m-long tail and weighing 70kg. They have a very powerful kick with their hind legs and are excellent boxers. In fact, a kangaroo could kick-box far better than Bruce Lee. A kangaroo kick is powerful enough to rip open your stomach!

Giant jumbo

The African elephant is the biggest land mammal living on Earth today. The biggest African elephant ever known

- weighed 12.2 tonnes (as heavy as a lorry)
- stood 3.96m high (as tall as a bungalow)
- was 9.75m long from trunk to tail (as long as a coach) and
- measured 3m from the tip of one ear to the tip of the other (bigger than your bedsheets).

Jumbo hunger

Elephants are always eating. An elephant eats around 200kg of food a day – that's the same as 1,760 beefburgers.

African elephants normally weigh about 6 or 7 tonnes – equal to more than 130 fully grown men.

Jumbo junior

A newborn baby elephant can weigh twice as much as your dad. It drinks 11 litres of milk every day.

Toothy grin

Imagine having teeth 3.3m long! That's the length of the longest tusks ever found on an elephant. The heaviest tusks ever seen weighed nearly 103kg – that's more than twice as heavy as you.

An elephant can lift up to 1 tonne with its tusks. That's about the same weight as a family saloon car.

An elephant's trunk contains 40,000 muscles! You only have 650 muscles in your entire body!

Rumbly jumbo

Elephants are very noisy animals. You can't hear them, but you can feel them coming up to 8km away. They send out a noisy, rumbling vibration that makes your bones quake.

17

Big ears

Elephants are giants in other ways, too. The African elephant has the biggest ears of any mammal. Each ear is the size of a tablecloth.

An elephant's intestines are 35m long – that's almost five times longer than yours. They would be as long as a string of more than 300 fat sausages.

Baby love

Never get between a mother elephant and its baby. The mother will think you mean to harm it. A protective mother elephant once chased a man through metal gates, overturned his car, lifted him high into the air, smashed him to the ground and then crushed him to a pulp.

GET THIS!

An elephant could fill a bath in just over a minute with seven squirts of water from its trunk and could drain more than three baths full of water in just over four minutes!

GET THIS!

In 1997, the remains of an entire woolly mammoth were found frozen in the Siberian ice. The remains have been stored in an icy underground cave where scientists hope to use part of its DNA to reproduce a living mammoth. If they are successful, a mammoth will walk the Earth for the first time in 10,000 years!

Mighty mammoths

Today's elephants are descended from the mammoth, a hairy monster that first lived 300,000 years ago. The biggest mammoth stood 4.5m high and had tusks 5m long. It would almost fill your house – upstairs and downstairs!

Heavyweight

A mammoth was immensely heavy and strong. A single mammoth weighed over 10 tonnes. Its tusks alone weighed the equivalent of a family fridge!

Super-shrew

We've had strong lions, tigers, kangaroos and elephants, but what about a mighty shrew? Believe it or not, the armoured shrew of Uganda has such a strong spine that a man could stand on its back. Yet this tiny shrew is just 15cm long.

GET THIS!

It was the fleas living on black rats that spread the Black Death plague in the 14th century, wiping out 75 million people in Europe and Asia. Rats carry the bacteria for at least five fatal diseases.

Ratless

The main enemy of the rat is the ferret. One ferret has been known to kill as many as 100 rats in a night!

Rats don't grow to huge sizes, but their South American cousin, the capybara, can grow to 1.4m long and weigh up to 66kg.

Lazybones!

The tree sloth of South America is the laziest creature on Earth. It spends almost all its time hanging upside down from branches and hardly ever moves. It's about the size of a dog, with long, shaggy fur.

The sloth never washes – so be warned! When it rains, its fur turns green because of an algae that lives in it.

It takes so long to digest its food that it only goes to the toilet once a week.

Although it can stand on its legs, the sloth doesn't use them, so it can't walk and, instead, has to drag itself along the ground. Yet it's a good swimmer – handy because it rains a lot in its South American home and the rivers there often flood.

Quill pain

The porcupine may have as many as 30,000 sharp quills on its back: that's about 40 for every patch the size of your thumbnail. If you annoy it, a porcupine will back into you and stab you with its quills. If you don't get it out quickly, a quill can work its way right through your leg!

Hog wash

The giant forest hog of central Africa can grow up to 2.5m long and weigh 275kg. That's as big as a cow!

Hippo hop

The hippo weighs up to 3,600kg and measures 1.6m high and 4.2m long – so it's as big and heavy as a fully laden Land Rover. Despite its size, it's an amazingly agile creature and can turn a circle in its own length. Perhaps Disney's portrayal of hippos as ballet dancers in the film *Fantasia* isn't far wrong!

Piles of poo

Hippos have big stomachs, up to 7m long. They eat up to 45kg of grass every night – that's like you or me eating 18 cabbages one after the other! All this food means they do huge piles of poo. Hippos usually go to the toilet in the river. If they go on land, the poo pile can be up to 1m high!

GET THIS!

People once thought that hippos sweat blood. In fact, they ooze a pinkish oil which keeps their skin cool, otherwise they can get sunburn!

Boared to death

The wild boar is an amazingly strong and fearless creature that will fight anything. The largest boars grow to 1.8m long and may weigh more than 300kg. Young boars can move at an astonishing speed of up to 50km/h.

No surrender

Boars have vicious tusks. If hunted, a boar is likely to charge its attacker rather than flee, and its speed and power mean that it would continue to run up the shaft of a lance even when speared!

Mega-stink

The skunk produces the foulest smelling liquid ever. If you get sprayed by a skunk it can cause temporary blindness, injure your nose and you remain stinky for over a year. Your friends would be able to smell you from 1.6km away!

King Kong

The biggest ever living gorilla weighed 310kg and measured nearly 2m round his chest. He'd have to wear pyjamas twice as large as your dad's.

GET THIS!

A gorilla may be about the same size as a man and about twice as heavy but it's about four times as strong as the strongest man. One gorilla could easily lift the equivalent of two family cars.

A gorilla could burst a football under its arms and turn a huge tractor tyre inside out. Yet, despite its strength, the gorilla is a very peaceable animal and likes to live a quiet life.

There has only been one reported case of a gorilla killing a human. The man must have caught the gorilla by surprise. The gorilla lifted the man from the ground and then pulled off his head and plucked out his arms – as easily as picking grapes off a bunch.

The orang-utan can stretch its long arms 2.5m wide. That means it could probably stretch from one wall to the other in your bedroom.

Noisy neighbours

Siamang gibbons make such a loud noise that anyone working with them is advised to wear ear-muffs to protect their ears! No one's told the gibbons, though!

Bigfoot

Some people have reported seeing a huge ape in North America, which they call Bigfoot or Sasquatch. They say it stood 2.4m high and took giant strides up to 3m long! And yes, it also had huge feet, each 43cm long.

Beastly baboons

Baboons are the most dangerous of all the apes. They have vicious teeth and could bite right through your wrist.

Female baboons are very protective, they have even been known to kidnap human babies.

Never turn your back on a baboon. They love to bite you on the bum – and their teeth are deadly sharp. Ouch!

Cheeky chimps

A fully grown chimpanzee can weigh 60kg. That's equal to about 300 bananas.

Chimpanzees aren't always as cuddly as you'd think. They will gang up and attack little monkeys, often pulling them apart.

Face-licking fun

The okapi has a monster tongue measuring 36cm long. This means an okapi can give its face a complete wash and even lick out its own ears. (I'd rather use a flannel myself!)

Monster tongue

At 45cm, the giraffe's tongue is even longer than that of the okapi. But the champion monster tongue of all belongs to the giant anteater. Its tongue is a staggering 61cm long. If your tongue was that long, you could lick your belly-button! What's more, the anteater darts its tongue in and out 160 times a minute.

Long horn

The longest horn ever seen on an Indian rhinoceros measured 1.5m. But a bull Asian water buffalo was once known to have had horns that spread 4.2m from tip to tip. That's probably the width of your living room at home.

Horrendous horns

The biggest antlers on any animal known today were on a moose. They measured 2m across.

Stripe code

No two zebras are alike. Every zebra's striped markings are different, just like a bar code. Zebras weigh up to 450kg and stand 1.6m high, making them the largest members of the horse family. They can run at speeds of 60km/h.

High horse

The biggest horse ever was Big Jim, a Clydesdale, which was 2.16m high at the shoulder and weighed over 1 tonne.

Shire horses are immensely strong. In 1893, a team of two horses pulled over 55 tonnes of logs on a sledge across snow.

Got the hump?

Camels have a reputation for always being grumpy. A camel moans and groans at anything it has to do, but it is still one of the most remarkable animals alive. Just think what a camel can do. It can

- go for 17 days without water.
- lose up to 27% of its body weight – or about 180kg – without ill effect.
- drink 100 litres of water in 10 minutes – that's $1\frac{1}{4}$ baths full!
- survive baking hot and freezing cold temperatures over a range of 50°C. (Once, a camel fell through an ice-covered lake and was in freezing water for half an hour, yet it survived.)
- carry up to 270kg of baggage – that's more than the weight of five average people – and travel fully loaded for 40km a day.
- travel 190km a day at a steady pace of 16km/h (if not carrying a load).
- continue to work like this for over 30 years.

Head in the trees

The giraffe is the tallest living creature thanks to its monster-long neck. Giraffes have been known to grow more than 6m, which is taller than a double-decker bus. A giraffe's neck alone can measure up to 3m.

A giraffe needs a big heart to pump blood up its long neck to its brain. A giraffe's heart is nearly 40 times bigger than your heart and weighs over 11kg.

The giraffe is also pretty heavy. It weighs up to 1,900kg, or nearly 2 tonnes. It eats 134kg of food (mostly leaves) every day. That's the same as you eating about 50 raw cabbages.

Despite its great weight and spindly legs, a giraffe could outrun any human. A galloping giraffe can reach speeds of up to 60km/h.

GET THIS!

Zarafa was a famous giraffe in France. She was shipped to Marseilles from Alexandria in 1826. She was so tall they had to cut a hole in the deck of the ship for her to put her head through. She then walked an amazing 885km right across France to Paris.

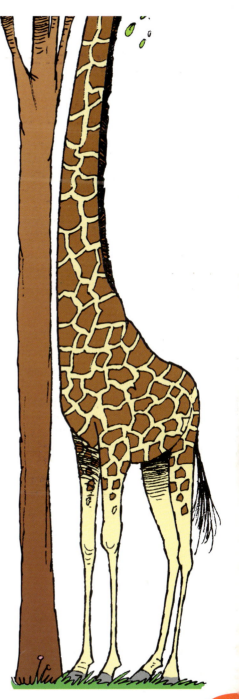

Cool bear

The biggest carnivore (meat-eater) in the world is the polar bear. A full-grown adult can weigh around 400kg and stand 2.4m high.

Bears are immensely strong. The greatest weight known to have been moved by a polar bear was 600kg, when it dragged away a white whale it had killed.

Icevisible

Polar bears have even been known to hide behind a block of ice and push the block forward so that they remain completely hidden as they stalk their prey.

Polathon

Polar bears are incredible swimmers and have been known to swim over 150km in search of prey. They can smell their prey over 20km away.

Bears will pursue their prey, including humans, for days over long distances. The Inuit believe that once a polar bear has chosen its prey, it hunts it to the end.

Big foot

Polar bears have huge feet, each around 30cm across. They'd have to wear size 12 boots with a very wide fitting!

Super seals

Although most seals are not much bigger than you or me, some seals are really huge. The elephant seals of the South Pole can grow 5m long and weigh over 2 tonnes! The biggest ever seen was over 6.8m long and weighed 4 tonnes, so it really was elephant-sized. It measured 5m around its waist, so if it ever needed to wear trousers, they'd have to be the size of a two-person tent!

GET THIS!

A polar bear's skin is black not white. And its fur isn't white either. It's colourless. It only looks white because of the way it reflects light.

Weighty walrus

Almost as big as the elephant seal is the walrus. A big bull walrus can weigh up to 3.5 tonnes and be up to 5.8m in length. If one came to stay, it would need two beds to sleep in.

It would also need to spend ages cleaning its teeth before it went to bed. A walrus's teeth, or tusks, can grow up to 1m long. That's the length of six large toothpaste tubes, laid end to end.

And wow, do walruses eat! Walruses loves clams and whelks and all kinds of molluscs. They dig them up with their tusks and eat as many as 3,000 in one meal.

COLD-BLOODED BEASTIES

Many reptiles and lizards are the descendants, or relatives, of the dinosaurs and some of them, such as the crocodile and the Komodo dragon, even look like dinosaurs.

In this section, you'll find some of the most dangerous and vicious of all creatures, including

- the most powerful jaws ever
- the most poisonous creature in the world
- the biggest dragon in the world
- a worm-tongued snip-snapper
- a lizard that runs on water

and plenty of other cold-blooded creatures that slither, stink, bite and stab.

Mind how you turn the page …

Ancient beasties

Tortoises are renowned for their old age, although few definite ages much beyond 110 have been recorded. The oldest tortoise known for certain lived to about 170 years. That's useful, because a tortoise takes a long time to get anywhere. In a hurry, it can only move about 330m in an hour.

The giant Galapagos tortoise can weigh over 350kg. Its shell is over 1m long.

The snip-snapper

The alligator snapping turtle is a fearsome beastie. The whole turtle weighs about 114kg and has a 66cm-long shell. Its head is as big as yours.

The snapping turtle lies on the bottom of rivers or lakes disguised as a rock, keeping its mouth wide open to reveal its worm-like tongue. Fish think the tip of the turtle's tongue is a tasty worm. When they swim over to eat it – snap! – the turtle's jaws clamp shut and snip the fish in half.

What's the mata?

The matamata is a small turtle that looks like a pineapple! It's so lazy that algae grow on its shell. It lies at the bottom of rivers. When a fish swims by, the matamata opens its mouth and sucks in the fish like a vacuum cleaner.

Big head

The big-headed turtle of Vietnam can't hide its head in its shell because it's too big. Instead, it has another shell on its head that looks rather like a crash helmet.

Stinky-pot

The stinkpot turtle of the United States is a real stinker. If threatened, it lets off a terrible stench, powerful enough to drive away its enemies.

GET THIS!

The police use snapping turtles to find dead bodies at the bottom of lakes. The turtles are good at sniffing out rotting flesh and then gripping it tightly … Yuck!

Creepy-crawlie lizard

Worm lizards look a bit like huge worms. Most worm lizards have no legs at all, but the odd two-legged worm lizard has a pair of legs at the front, which it uses to dig tunnels. These lizards are bright pink and look a bit like giant fingers crawling through the soil.

The glass snake isn't a snake at all. It's a kind of legless lizard, like the slow worm. The glass snake grows up to 1.5m long. Half its length is its tail. If attacked, the tail can split into several pieces to confuse the attacker while the rest of the snake's body and head slither away to safety.

Stand and deliver

The galliwasp isn't a wasp but a lizard. It likes to eat bird poo and vomit. It will attack sea birds returning with food for their chicks. This makes the sea bird vomit up the food it's carrying, which the galliwasp then eats.

Poisonous heela

Despite its name, the Gila monster is quite small, growing to about 60cm long at most. It is one of just two types of poisonous lizard in the whole world.

Shy but deadly

Gila monsters are shy and won't attack unless provoked but when they do, their bite is very dangerous. One in three people bitten by a Gila monster dies.

GET THIS!

Gila monsters are greedy things. They can eat a third of their body weight in a single meal (usually made up of small insects and birds' eggs). Can you imagine eating over 200 fried eggs in one sitting? Because they eat so much in one go, they really only need four or five hearty meals to last them all year!

Monster dragon

The biggest lizard in the world – and the closest-looking creature to a living dinosaur – is the Komodo dragon of Indonesia. These beasts can be over 3m long and weigh 165kg.

They love to burrow their way into their victim when eating it, so Komodo dragons are often covered in blood, guts and slime during dinner.

Komodo dragons can eat almost their own weight in food in one meal. One dragon ate a 30kg boar in 17 minutes. You would have to eat 260 beefburgers or 600 sausages in the same length of time to beat that!

I'm bigger than you!

The frill-necked lizard of Australia likes to pretend it's bigger than it really is. It has huge frills of skin on either side of its head, which it flaps out like wings that stretch up to 25cm wide. This makes it look rather like it has stuck its head through a tablecloth.

A frill-necked lizard will often stand on its hind legs and fight other frill-necked lizards, each trying to look the most frightening. Sounds like just another day in the school playground!

At 7.5cm long, the flying-dragon lizard is smaller than your hand but it can glide over 60m between treetops. To fly, it stretches out two flaps of skin on either side of its body like a pair of wings.

Break-dancer

The sand-diving lizard lives in the hottest parts of the Namib Desert in Africa. The sand gets so hot that the lizard could easily burn its feet. When it's standing, it hops up and down, lifting alternate feet, in a bizarre 'thermal' dance so that its feet don't touch the hot sand for long.

Speed machine

The basilisk lizard of South America, is only a little fellow (well, 80cm long) but it has such big feet and can skuttle along on its hind legs so fast (at about 11km/h) that it can run over water for up to 40m.

Prickly larder

The thorny devil of Australia is a lizard covered in spiky knobs. It has the wonderful scientific name of *Moloch horridus*. This lizard can eat up to 1,800 ants at a time. When it rains, it stores water between its scales. When it needs a drink, it drains the water to its mouth along little canals.

Eye-eye

Tuataras are rare reptile survivors from the days before the dinosaurs and have been around for 200 million years. They look like lizards but they're not. They have no living relatives left on Earth. A tuatara has a third eye on top of its head. As it grows, this 'eye' is covered over by scales. Scientists are not sure what it is used for. Any ideas?

Puff-daddy

Can you inflate like a balloon? The American chuckwalla lizard can. It puffs up its lungs to three times their size and wedges itself into holes in the rock so nothing can get at it.

Bleeding nuisance

If the Texas horned lizard is threatened, it changes colour, puffs itself up and then squirts blood from its eyes up to 1m into the air! Now that would soon scare off any enemies.

Swimming in sand

The sandfish isn't a fish at all but another type of lizard. It has adapted to living in sand so well, it moves through it as though it were swimming.

The sandfish is a species of skink. Yes, skink – that's not a misprint for skunk. The skink is one of the most common lizards. One of them, the spiny-tailed skink, is pinkish in colour. In fact, it looks like a long pink gherkin. It's a shame it doesn't smell, too, so we could call it the spiny stinky pink skink! Try saying *that* quickly.

Tongue-tastic

The chameleon has a 20-cm long, sticky tongue, which it shoots out at great speed to catch insects. Since a chameleon is usually only about 15cm long, its tongue is longer than its body!

The tip of a chameleon's tongue can travel at up to 5m/sec or 18km/h, which is faster than you can run.

The chameleon is known for being able to change colour and blend in with its surroundings. Imagine what fun hide and seek would be if you could simply turn green in the garden!

Big crocs

The biggest crocodile ever lived 70 million years ago and is called *Deinosuchus* (die-no-sook-us) which means 'terrible crocodile'. It grew up to 15m long and had 2m-long jaws. It could have swallowed you easily in just one gulp, including your sooks (sorry, socks).

After a crocodile has eaten, it usually goes to sleep with its mouth wide open. Birds then fly down and clean the crocodile's teeth by picking out and eating any bits of flesh. Imagine if a budgie came to clean your teeth while you slept …

GET THIS!

In just one night in 1945, crocodiles are believed to have killed and eaten almost 1,000 men trapped on a small island off the coast of Burma.

Giant jaws

Crocodiles are the largest reptiles living in the world and among the most dangerous of all creatures. The biggest crocodile lives in India and is called the saltwater crocodile. If it stood on its nose, the tip of its tail would be almost as tall as a house. These crocs grow over 8m long and weigh around 2,000kg.

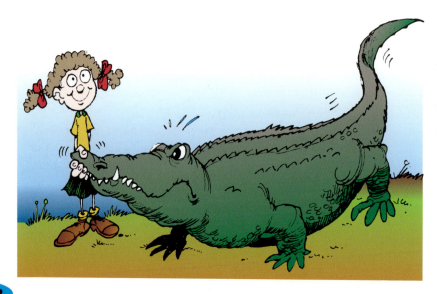

Giant battle

Crocodiles will attack any animal and have been known to kill baby elephants and old hippos. Only a big bull elephant is strong enough to defeat a crocodile – a real battle of the giants.

Snappy

A crocodile's jaws are vicious. They snap shut with a force of 1,360kg – that's 17 times more powerful than your jaws and probably rather like having a large car dropped on your head. Crocs can run much faster than you, too, at up to 50km/h.

GET THIS!

Crocodiles find it harder to open their jaws than shut them, so you could hold a crocodile's jaws shut with one hand (assuming it hasn't eaten the other one!).

Smile please!

You can tell an alligator from a crocodile from the way it shuts its jaws. When shut, a crocodile's teeth are all in line, but an alligator's upper teeth close outside the lower teeth. In other words, a crocodile smiles but an alligator grits its teeth. I wouldn't try and get close enough to see for yourself though – use binoculars instead!

The biggest-ever alligator was 5.84m long. That's almost as long as two cars.

Frog-tastic

The biggest frog in the world is the Goliath frog of West Africa. When fully stretched, it is over 80cm long and weighs 3.3kg. It looks rather like a big brown grapefruit with arms and legs.

The world's largest toad, the marine toad of South America, isn't as big as the Goliath frog but it makes up for it by looking more gruesome as it's covered in warts.

Don't touch me!

Keep away from the poison-arrow frog of South America. Its Latin name is *Phyllobates terribilis* because it is so poisonous. It's only tiny but its body oozes enough poison to kill 20,000 people! Just 1g of its poison could kill 90,000 people!

Other frogs have disgusting ways of keeping people away.
- The Venezuelan skunk frog is the smelliest creature in the world. It stinks like a skunk and can be smelled from 1.6km away.
- If you pick up the Japanese dagger frog it will stab you with its thumb.
- The spadefoot toad of Germany stinks of garlic!

GET THIS!

The fire salamander got its name because people once wrongly believed that the salamander could not be harmed by fire. This idea probably started because salamanders would crawl out from under logs used in bonfires.

Toadcake

The Surinam toad is almost completely flat. It's up to 18cm long but less than 2cm thick. It looks like a pancake with legs.

The female Surinam toad lays her eggs on her back. The eggs look like lots of tiny tablets. The eggs hatch into tadpoles and stay on the mother's back in little pockets of leathery lace until they become froglets.

Gift-wrapped

The water-holding frog lives in the Australian desert. To avoid the Sun, it spends most of its time buried under the ground wrapped in skin like a plastic bag. It only comes out when it rains.

Teenage tadpole

Some creatures have wonderful names. How about the axolotl. Axolotl is an Aztec name meaning 'water monster'. It's really a salamander that has never grown up. It keeps its gills and stays in water, rather like a giant tadpole. It only grows up if it has to – for example, if its pond dries up. Then it develops legs and marches off to find another pond.

Although weird, the axolotl is quite cute. Another creature that doesn't like growing up is much more savage. The Congo eel (a salamander, despite its name) may grow up to 90cm long and has strong vicious teeth.

What a babe!

When the olm or cave salamander was discovered for the first time, it was thought to be a baby dragon.

The biggest salamander in the world is the Chinese giant salamander. The largest ever known of these big beasts grew to 1.8m long and weighed 65kg, which is around the size of a small crocodile.

45

S-s-s-slithery s-s-s-snakes

Just imagine millions of writhing and wriggling snakes. The most snakes ever seen together were Astratia sea snakes. A whole slick of them 3m wide and over 100km long was once seen writhing in the sea … Nice!

Revenge

The natural enemy of the cobra is the mongoose, which looks like a 1m-long ferret. It's so agile, it can move more quickly than the cobra can strike. The mongoose pounces on the snake and crushes the snake's skull. If it is too slow, the snake will bite and kill it. It really is a fight to the death.

Slime defence

The snail-eating snake lives in South America. The snake takes a deep breath then forces its upper jaw into the shell of a snail. It needs to take in air because the snail fights back by producing lots and lots of slime, which it pushes into the snake's mouth to stop it breathing!

Fang-tastic

Big snakes may crush you but the ones to watch out for are the poisonous snakes. More people die every year from snake bites than from all the other animal-related deaths put together.

GET THIS!

Every autumn over 20,000 red garter snakes travel 16km from the marshes of Manitoba in Canada to the safety of the rocky caves, and every spring they make the return trip. They make the same journey every year even if it means going through people's houses!

Crushmungus

The biggest slithery snake in the world is the anaconda of South America. Anacondas measuring up to 24m have been seen in the wild but never captured. The biggest ever caught was

- 8.5m long (as long as two cars)
- 1.1m thick (as wide as a large man's waist)
- and weighed 227kg (five times heavier than you)

… that's big!

An anaconda could swallow as many as ten people, though it's unlikely ever to do that. Anacondas do swallow entire pigs or small deer whole. The creature then dissolves in the anaconda's gut!

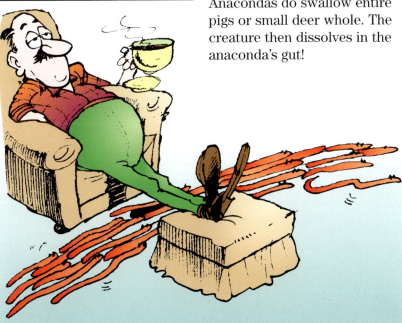

BEASTIES OF THE

DEEP

Over 70% of the Earth's surface is covered by water, and some of the oceans are very, very deep. We've hardly begun to explore the ocean depths. Who knows what undiscovered monsters may be lurking down there …

In this chapter, you can discover what we **do** know about these giants of the seas. You'll read about

- the biggest animal in the world, ever
- the most savage living creatures
- lots of long and wriggly tentacles
- the biggest and fastest mouths
- brainless blobs
- sea serpents
- the worst pain in the world!

and a whole lot more that's wet, wild and wicked.

Whopping whales

The biggest animal ever – bigger even than the biggest dinosaur – is the blue whale. It can grow up to 33m long and weigh up to 150 tonnes. That's as heavy as 2,800 children. It's like a small village!

The blue whale is so big there is no way it could live on land. It would be crushed by the weight of its own body. It survives in the ocean because its great weight is supported by the water.

Everything about a blue whale is huge.

- Its tongue weighs as much as an elephant.
- It has 8,500 litres of blood – that's nearly 2,000 times as much as you have.
- When it opens its mouth, it can drink up to 1,000 tonnes of water in one gulp – that's as much as four normal-sized swimming pools full of water.
- And wow, is it noisy! It can make noises one-and-a-half times louder than a jet plane taking off. Both the blue whale and the finback whale can communicate over distances of up to 850km with sounds so high-pitched they can't be heard by humans.

What's for afters?

Whales eat 40 million krill a day, but that's no problem. Krill are found in massive swarms. The biggest-ever swarm weighed 10 million tonnes. That's enough to feed all the blue whales in the world for over eight months.

Deep-sea diver

The sperm whale can blow air and water through the blowhole on the top of its head up to 15m into the air.

Sperm whales also dive as deep as 3,000m under the sea. They can remain under the water for up to two hours – and all without a snorkel. This is quite a feat. Remember – whales are mammals and need to breathe air.

At these depths, sperm whales pursue giant squid as their main food. Some whales bear the scars of battles with these squid – something no human has ever seen. Now that would be a real monster fight!

GET THIS!

Each sperm whale tooth is about 18cm long and weighs 900g – about as much as a bag of sugar. Sperm whales have about 50 teeth, all in their lower jaw. The total weight of all these teeth is around 45kg, or about as heavy as you.

Headbanger

The bowhead whale can burst its way through ice 30cm thick without getting a headache!

Thick-skinned?

The beautiful white beluga whales of the Arctic have skin 1cm thick – that's five times thicker than your skin. The Inuit call this skin *muktuk*. (Sounds like a dirty dinner to me!)

Smile please

The bowhead whale has a huge mouth. Its mouth makes up one-third of its 20m-long body.

A whale of a dart

The narwhal is the unicorn of the sea. The male narwhal grows up to 5m long and has a further 2.7m of tusk on the front of its head. This is a formidable weapon as the narwhal can spear its tusk up to 60cm into another whale. (It must be good at darts.)

Brainy Dick

Have you ever heard of Moby Dick, a great white whale? Well, Moby Dick was a sperm whale, and sperm whales have the biggest brains in the animal kingdom. A sperm whale's brain weighs 10kg, which is over six times heavier than your brain. But is it six times smarter than you? That depends on how clever you are!

The sperm whale is not as big as the blue whale but is still very large. It can grow up to 20m long and weigh over 60 tonnes, and it has huge teeth. Its bottom jaw alone measures 5m.

GET THIS!

Orcas can leap up to 8m out of the water and crash back with such a splash that the noise can be heard 8km away.

Mighty orca

The orca, or killer whale, is the real ruler of the seas. This massive creature, closely related to the dolphin, can weigh 10 tonnes and is about 10m long. It can move at speeds of up to 55km/h.

Orcas have the second-largest brains in the animal kingdom, but are more intelligent than the larger-brained sperm whale. Orcas have been known to kill even great white sharks but they've never been known to kill a human.

GET THIS!

A baby blue whale is as heavy as an elephant when it is born. It can weigh up to 7 tonnes and grows at the rate of nearly 5kg an hour. The largest babies can drink 600 litres of their mother's milk every day.

Savage sharks?

Most sharks are quite safe and will not hurt humans. This includes the largest shark of them all, the whale shark, which can grow up to 18m long and weigh around 43 tonnes. The whale shark is the biggest fish in the world. You could easily swim in and out of its mouth.

Another huge fish is the basking shark. This usually grows up to 12m long and weighs up to 8 tonnes, though the biggest ever was rumoured to be 13.7m long and weigh 14.5 tonnes.

Hammer-plane

The hammerhead shark can grow to over 6m in length. Despite its name, it wouldn't be much use at hammering in nails. It looks a bit like a shark pretending to be an aeroplane. Its head is wing-shaped and it has one eye at the end of each wing.

GET THIS!

In 1942, a British ship was torpedoed and 900 sailors and prisoners of war were thrown into the water, clinging to the wreckage. Before they could be rescued, over 700 of them were eaten by sharks!

Sharp smell

Sharks have an awesome sense of smell. They can detect one tiny drop of blood in over 100 million drops of water from up to 5km away. That's almost as incredible as you being in London and smelling your socks in Birmingham!

Big gobs

The basking shark can swallow over 1.8 million litres of water an hour – about as much water as there is in an Olympic-sized swimming pool. Basking sharks can open their jaws more than 2m wide and could easily swallow a dolphin whole.

There is a shark whose mouth is so big, it's called the megamouth shark. The mouth is the size of a bathtub and the inside glows in the dark, luring deep-sea fish to their doom.

Woebegone wobbegong

Don't make fun of the wobbegong shark, even though it does appear to wear frilly knickers around its mouth. It easily gets annoyed. The tasselled wobbegong lurks in caves and will attack anything that annoys it.

Killer sharks

The most fearsome of all sharks is the great white shark. The biggest ever known was 7.6m long and weighed about 770kg, but people say they have seen great whites up to 11m long. These sharks have been known to swallow seals (or even small dolphins) whole.

The most dangerous shark to humans is the bull shark. This is because it swims in rivers and lakes, so it gets closer to where humans live. The bull shark isn't as big as the great white, growing up to 3.4m long, but it is ferocious and has been known to eat not only turtles and dolphins but antelope, dogs, humans and even tree sloths.

Can-opening cookie

At 50cm, the cookie-cutter shark is quite small, but it has a nasty bite. It clamps its sucker-like lips on to its victim and then spins round, cutting out a neat cookie-shaped circle of flesh, just like opening a can of baked beans!

GET THIS!

The great white shark has up to 3,000 teeth arranged in rows. You have 32. (No contest there!) If a shark's teeth fall out, new ones grow in their place, so sharks never need a set of false teeth! During its lifetime, a tiger shark may grow and lose over 24,000 teeth.

Vicious fishes

The piranha fish of South America is the most vicious fish in the world. A piranha can grow up to 60cm long and has teeth like razors. It feeds in groups and is attracted by the smell of blood. A shoal of piranha has been known to pull an entire buffalo into a river and eat it within 10 minutes.

Big nose

The longnose gar fish has a 30cm-long snout, which is about one-fifth the length of its body. Its mouth contains loads of sharp, needle-like teeth, and it has a second set of teeth at the entrance to its stomach.

The scales of this fish are so strong that the Native American people used them as arrowheads. Hopefully, they didn't fire the whole fish at their enemies!

The alligator gar can grow up to 3m long and has vicious teeth. It sometimes skims along the surface of the water chasing its prey. If you swam in its way, you could get speared!

GET THIS!

In 1981, 300 people were eaten alive by piranhas when their boat capsized off the coast of Brazil.

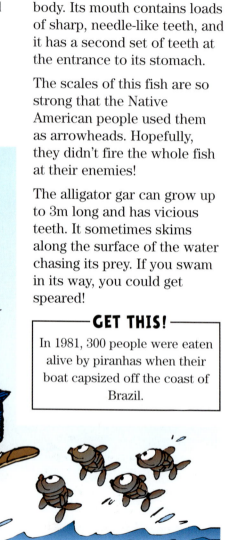

Sea serpent

The oarfish is a bizarre creature. It has a long, thick body, like that of a snake, large eyes and a dragon-like face. It has a crest along its back and swims by rippling along. The longest oarfish ever recorded was 17m. It is thought that it may be the basis for many of the mysterious stories about sea serpents.

Take a bite

Don't wave at a barracuda. It won't wave back; it'll attack you. And, at 2m long and up to 50kg in weight, a barracuda is much bigger than you and could eat the flesh off your leg in seconds. It can also swim five times faster than you – so there's no escape!

Big puff

A puffer fish can grow up to 50cm long. When threatened, it sucks in water and blows itself up into a round ball covered in sharp spikes. The puffer fish is also highly poisonous. That doesn't stop the Japanese eating it as a delicacy, though. Although chefs remove its poison first, about 100 people a year die from eating puffer fish.

Leaving home

If the walking catfish gets tired of its surroundings, it simply packs its bags and leaves. When these fish were first introduced into Florida, the fishponds soon became overcrowded, so the catfish just left and walked to the local river!

Carp a load of this

Some koi carp grow up to 1m in length but the biggest carp, the mahseer, can grow to as much as 3m long and weigh 54kg. Try keeping **that** in your fish tank!

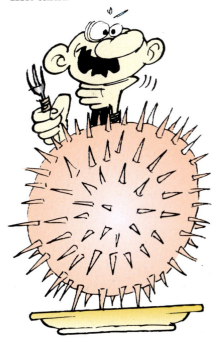

Greedy gobbler

Bluefish – which you find in most seas – are monster predators. They grow up to 1.2m long and swim in gangs. Bluefish attack and kill far more fish than they can eat, but they have a good try. They swallow 40 fish at a time, vomit them out, then start over again!

Light meal

The deep-sea viperfish lures other fish towards it with a light that glows in a fin over its head. The viperfish has long fangs, and expandable jaws so that it can clamp its fangs around particularly large victims.

Mighty mouth

The black swallower fish can eat fish two or three times its own size. Its mouth and body simply inflate like a balloon.

The wolf-fish can grow up to 2m long. Its teeth are so strong, it can leave bite marks on a ship's anchor.

Slime bags

The hagfish looks like a 60cm-long, slimy sausage covered in mucus. A hagfish will bore its way into a dead or dying fish and eat everything inside except the bones. Hagfish can eat 18 times their own weight in just 7 hours. Just one hagfish creates so much slime, it could fill a bucket within a couple of days.

The parrotfish of the Caribbean blows itself a bubble of mucus at night and goes to sleep in it. The mucus tastes awful, so other fish leave it alone while it sleeps in peace in its slimy sleeping bag!

Bum-cumber

What's grey, looks like a slug pretending to be a cucumber, and when threatened spits its guts at you? The sea cucumber, that's what! This creature is related to the starfish and can grow up to 1m long. Now that's a lot of cucumber!

The sea cucumber's mouth and bum are together in one hole. Yuck!

Frozen fish

There are fish that live in water colder than your refrigerator. The Antarctic cod has a special type of anti-freeze in its blood.

The icefish has thick white blood. When cut, it bleeds pus. Yuck!

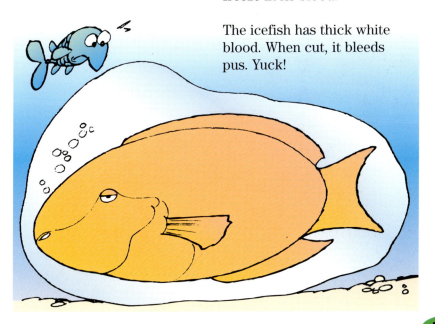

Pee on poison poisson

The most poisonous fish is the stonefish. It's easy to tread on a stonefish because it blends in with its surroundings. Its poison can kill but usually drives the person mad with pain first. Once bitten, a leg may swell up to twice its normal size. A stonefish bite is supposed to be the worst pain ever. One way to get relief is to pee on the wound, as hot water helps to reduce the pain.

> **GET THIS!**
> The sea urchin has been known to drill its way through steel 2cm thick.

Choose your weapon

The sawfish is related to the ray but looks more like a hedge trimmer. You'd have trouble lifting it, though. It's up to 8m long and can weigh 276kg – the weight of five men! It has a 2m-long snout lined with up to 64 teeth that grow outwards. Its saw-like snout can inflict tremendous damage.

The swordfish is much heavier. It grows up to 4.9m long and can weigh 450kg. Its sword-like snout can grow 1.4m long, and it can ram its snout through more than 50cm of wood at a speed of up to 96km/h.

Brainless blob

The jellyfish is a strange creature. It has eyes but no brain! Yet these brainless blobs can grow huge and even kill people.

The biggest jellyfish ever known is the Arctic lion's mane. The bowl-like jelly part, which floats in the water, is 2.28m across – that's almost as big as a car. It has 1,200 tentacles, each up to 36.5m long, or longer than all but the biggest whales. Spread out, the tentacles would cover an area as large as a tennis court. Yet this immense creature is 98% water!

The Arctic lion's mane is poisonous, but the most poisonous jellyfish of all is the sea wasp (also called the box jellyfish), which floats off the coast of Australia. The sea wasp is as big as a basketball and has 60 tentacles that are more than 4.5m long. If one stings you, it could kill you in less than a minute.

GET THIS!

A few years ago, a houndfish jumped out of the water and speared a fisherman through his leg!

BUT GET THIS!

Amazingly, the sting of the sea wasp doesn't penetrate thick tights. So if you go swimming in thick woolly stockings and a jumper you should be safe from the sting!*
* But I wouldn't try it!

Exploding hedgehogs

If you thought the monster in the film *Alien* was fiction, think again. The sea urchin looks a lot like the land hedgehog and is covered in sharp spines. If it gets swallowed by a shark (which happens often), the sea urchin inflates itself until the spines stick through the shark's stomach lining. It then rips itself an opening and swims free!

Turtle power

Another whopper of the seas is the leatherback turtle. The biggest ever known had a shell measuring nearly 3m long. The whole animal weighed almost 1 tonne, about as much as a car.

Normally, leatherback turtles are about 2.2m across and weigh about 450kg. That's still bigger than the world's biggest tortoise, the Galapagos tortoise, which weighs around 400kg and is about 1.3m long.

GET THIS!

The shell of a turtle is amazingly strong. It can support a weight over 200 times heavier than its body. That would be like you having nine cars on your back.

Octacles

If you were stupid enough to play with the Australian blue-ringed octopus, it could kill you in less than two hours. Although it's only 15cm long, its beak has a deadly poisonous bite.

The giant deep-sea octopus can grow to lengths of 20m. It could turn on the TV in the lounge, have a bite to eat in the kitchen and play ping-pong with itself in the garden – all at the same time. (And probably leer into the fish tank while it's at it!)

GET THIS!

The female octopus can lay up to 150,000 eggs. She looks after the eggs for six weeks and then, when they hatch, she dies.

Factopus octs

Here are some other amazing octopus facts:

- It is highly intelligent.
- It has three hearts.
- It moves by jet propulsion.
- It changes colour to blend in with its surroundings.
- When frightened, it squirts out black ink to hide in so it can make its escape.

R—eel shockers

The South American paroque eel, found in the Amazon, can produce an electric shock of up to 650 volts. That's enough to kill a horse and to power a microwave oven. This slithery shocker can grow up to 1.8m long and weighs 40kg.

Bigger and more vicious is the conger eel, which is usually about 2m long and weighs 50kg. It looks rather like the exploded tyre of a huge truck.

Some moray eels can grow even longer – up to 3m – but are lighter, at about 8kg. They look a lot like slippery hosepipes. They have vicious dagger-like teeth and strong jaws, and will attack you if you disturb them.

Shell shockers

Try lifting the giant clam. You'll need more muscle than mussel. A giant clam can weigh over 340kg and measure more than 1.1m across. You could go to bed comfortably in its shell, curled up with its huge 7kg pearls. Some giant clams are over 100 years old.

GET THIS!
The giant clam has the biggest foot of any living creature, at over 1.15m long! It would need an enormous sock and a size 112 shoe!

Living fossils

The coelacanth (see-la-kanth) was once thought to have died out 65 million years ago. It was rediscovered in 1938 living in the seas off the East African coast. Coelacanth are large, growing up to 1.8m long and weighing 98kg.

Large lungs

Coelacanth are closely related to lungfish. Lungfish have lungs as well as gills so can come out of water and breathe air. It's the only way they can survive when rivers and lakes dry out during hot summers.

The African lungfish is bigger than you, growing up to 2m long. Its lungs are better than its gills so it has to surface about once every half an hour to breathe otherwise it would drown! Perhaps it ought to wear a snorkel.

Sponge jam

Sponges are amazing. I'm talking about marine sponges, which are living animals, not jam sponges. You could pass a marine sponge through a grater and the individual bits would reform into one sponge. You couldn't do that with a jam sponge now, could you?

Scary sponge

In the deep, dark oceans there is a sponge that eats other animals, such as crabs. The sponge traps an animal in its spongy filaments and then gradually absorbs it. Errrgh!

Monsters of the twilight zone

Far down in the deepest oceans, where the light barely reaches, live some of the world's most fearsome fish. These fish are not large. If they were, they could not survive the meganormous pressure at this great depth (enough to squish you flat). Many of them, though, are vicious hunters.

- The female black dragonfish is virtually invisible in the dark but has a glowing piece of flesh that hangs from her lower jaw. This attracts tiny fish, which are promptly speared by the dragonfish's scores of sharp, needle-like teeth, then gobbled up.

- The baby dragonfish has eyes on stalks that float several centimetres above its body.

- The viperfish has teeth in its lower jaw that are so long, they jut up over its face.

- The female deep-sea anglerfish can grow up to 50cm long. It has a huge mouth full of vicious teeth like prison bars and a long glowing nose that writhes with tentacles.

And, just imagine, there could be even more weird monsters down there, waiting to be discovered …

FLAP-MUNGUS BEASTIES

Wouldn't it be wonderful to leap into the air and fly, like Superman? Of course it would! But don't try it or you'll fall flat on your face. Humans need special wings to fly, but birds and bats and insects have been flying for millions of years. And some of these flapping creatures are truly beautiful beasties. In this section, you'll find

- giant birds
- the featherweight champion of the world
- real bully birds
- the noisiest bird in the world
- the best bird football player
- vampires – the real things!

AND lots of other FLAP-MUNGUS beasties.

Jumbo birds

The biggest bird that ever lived was the Aepyornis, also called the 'elephant bird'. These jumbo birds used to live on the island of Madagascar. They stood over 3m high, and could weigh up to 500kg, or half a tonne.

Elephant birds laid the biggest eggs. Each egg was larger than a dinner plate (or 7 times bigger than an ostrich egg), weighed over 8kg and contained almost 10 litres of liquid – about the same amount held by your washing-up bowl!

The really big elephant birds lived tens of thousands of years ago, but their descendants, the moa, lived until recently. Arab sailors saw them in Madagascar and believed they could carry elephants away. They called them rocs.

GET THIS!

The moa survived in New Zealand until around 1850. Although not as heavy as the elephant bird, it was taller, at up to 3.5m high.

Isn't it sad that humans wiped these animals out in the last few centuries so that we don't get the pleasure of seeing them today?

Wandering wonder

Albatrosses are the giant wanderers of the world. They can fly for months at a time, sleeping on the wing.

An albatross spends 80% of its life flying. Just imagine spending almost 20 hours a day walking. One albatross was recorded as flying almost 40,000 kilometres in 90 days back and forth across the North Pacific Ocean looking for food for its chick. That's the same as flying from London to Newcastle every day for 90 days.

Jumbo wings

The frigate bird has a wingspan of almost 2.5m, nearly three times the length of its body.

Spread-eagle

The largest eagle is the harpy eagle of South America. Its wingspan is 3m and its body is over 1m long. It is immensely strong and has huge claws. It has been known to snatch sloths out of trees, even though these furry beasts weigh as much as the eagle, at about 5kg. Some of the larger harpies weigh up to 9kg.

Monkey eater

The harpy eagle is related to the monkey-eating eagle of the Philippines. This massive bird builds its nest 30m up in trees and will swoop down and snatch lemurs as they leap from tree to tree.

Flapping heck

The biggest living bird that can get off the ground is the great bustard. It looks a bit like a small turkey and weighs about 20kg – that's about the same weight you were when you were six years old.

That's a lot of weight to get off the ground so the bustard has to run and run and run and flap and flap and flap to get up enough speed. It does have huge wings to help, though, at up to 2.5m across!

Swan-upping

Almost as heavy as the bustard is the swan. This haughty heavyweight can weigh up to 15kg but it also has wings, up to 2.4m across. A swan has to reach a speed of 50km/h running on water before it can take off.

Don't tread on my feathers!

The phoenix fowl of Japan would be hopeless at playing hide-and-seek. This chicken-sized bird has a tail of feathers that stretch out over 10m behind it. Just imagine if your hair was so long it was still coming in the front door as you went out of the back!

Squirty-poos!

The potoo bird of the American tropics has brilliant camouflage and can disguise itself as a tree. So that it doesn't give away its whereabouts when it goes to the toilet, it has an incredible ability to squirt its poo up to several metres away. So, remember: avoid the potoo for fear of potoo poo!

Hot turkey

Don't argue with the turkey vulture. If anything tries to steal the dinner of this large American bird it vomits over them. And when it gets hot it pees down its legs to keep cool. Not the nicest bird to have on a perch in your living room.

This disgusting bird has a remarkable sense of smell. It can sense the smallest amount of rotting meat from well over a kilometre away.

Dicky-poo

The hoatzin bird of South America is a real stinker. It eats lots of fruit and leaves which ferment in its body, making the bird constantly smell of cow poo.

Big mouth

The toucan is a small bird with a monster beak. Sometimes its beak is bigger than the rest of the bird. Good job it's thin and light, otherwise the toucan would fall flat on its beak!

The biggest beak (or, to be more accurate, bill) is that of the pelican. This is a giant bird all round. Some pelicans stand up to 1.8m high and have a wingspan of 3m. A pelican's bill can be up to 50cm long and can hold up to 13 litres of water – that's more than your washing-up bowl.

The sword-billed hummingbird of South America is only 7cm long but has a 10cm-long beak, which it plunges into flowers to reach the sweet nectar inside. On the same scale, you would have a 2m-long nose (like Pinocchio).

Fierce frigates

The frigate bird is a proper bully. Although it does catch its own fish it finds it easier to steal fish from other birds. It will chase them until they drop their catch, then it grabs the fish in mid-air. It's impossible to escape the frigate bird. It is a remarkable flyer and can twist and turn and dive as well as it can fly, all at speeds up to 154km/h. In fact, it's the world's second-fastest bird, beaten only by the swift which can fly at 171km/h.

Flightless footballers

The ostrich is the biggest living bird and is as heavy as a fridge, at around 150kg. It stands 2.7m tall – as high as the cross-bar in a football goal.

Ostriches would make excellent footballers. They have a keen eye and can run very fast, at around 70km/h. But don't get one angry. An ostrich's kick is hefty enough to break your back.

An ostrich egg is huge – 20 times bigger than a chicken's egg.

Tall boy

Some cranes can fly even though they may grow 2m tall – that's taller than Superman!

GET THIS!

The swan has more feathers than any other bird – over 25,000 – making it the featherweight champion of the world!

Bullet birds

The peregrine falcon not only has good eyesight but can move at amazing speeds. When it dives to swoop on its victim, it can be moving at 298km/h – that's at one-quarter the speed of sound!

Other birds also dive better than Superman! The booby spots its fish from over 30m in the air. Then it folds its wings and darts down, hitting the sea at almost 100km/h. The shock wave under the water stuns any fish within 2m. The booby can travel almost 2m underwater and stay under for up to 40 seconds.

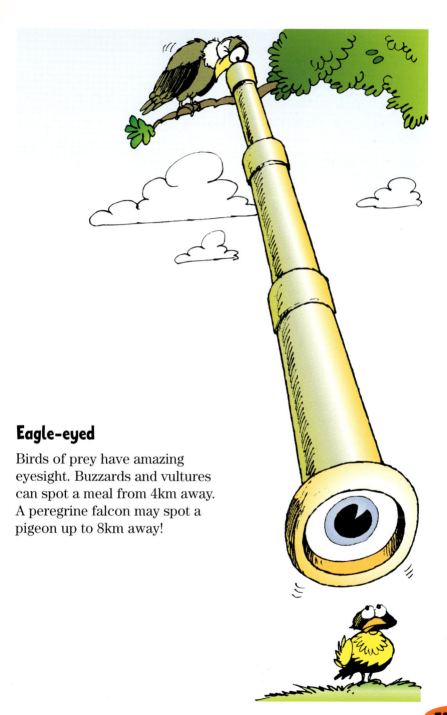

Eagle-eyed

Birds of prey have amazing eyesight. Buzzards and vultures can spot a meal from 4km away. A peregrine falcon may spot a pigeon up to 8km away!

Monster squatter

The cuckoo is notorious for laying its eggs in the nests of other birds. You'd think the other bird would notice, because the cuckoo's eggs are usually larger than its own, and sometimes a different colour, but the host bird continues to look after the egg and raises the infant cuckoo, even though the young cuckoo will have thrown any other baby birds out of the nest.

The young cuckoo grows quickly and is often much bigger than the host bird, which continues to feed it until it's old enough to fly away.

Monster flocks

The most common bird in the world is the quelea of Africa. Estimates range from 10 billion to 100 billion birds. They flock in their millions. So many will land in one tree at once that they break down the branches with their weight. One flock may weigh 200,000kg, or as much as 30 elephants.

The main benefit of quelea birds is their poo, called guano, which helps to fertilise the soil.

Home sweet home

The mallee fowl of Australia is a compulsive home-builder. Its nest is so big it keeps the eggs warm without Mum having to sit on them. Most nests are as big as a bungalow, at 4.6m high, 11m wide and weighing over 300 tonnes. It's a good job the mallee fowl builds its nest on the ground rather than in a tree!

Bald builder

The American bald eagle also makes a monster home, only this time high up in the trees. One tree eventually fell down with the weight of its nest. It weighed nearly 2 tonnes and was 2.6m wide and 3.7m deep. That's probably about the size of your bedroom!

Monster memory

Do you always remember where you left things? Clarke's nutcracker can. In November each year, it buries up to 30,000 pine seeds over an area of 500 sq km – that's an area as big as London. Over the winter, it digs these up again as it needs them and can find up to 27,000 of them, even when buried under snow. Could you do that?

Batty bat

The biggest bat is called a flying fox. It isn't a fox, although its face does look a bit fox-like. The flying fox is really a fruit bat. It has a wingspan of up to 1.8m, which is about as much as you with your arms stretched out.

Some people are scared of bats, but remember – bats are harmless and should be protected. I feel sorry for bats, eating all that fruit and then hanging upside down to sleep . . . I just hope they don't get diarrhoea.

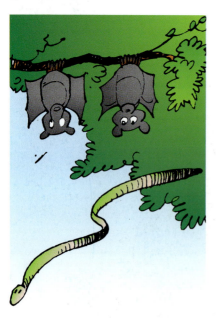

Vampires

When we think of vampires we think of Count Dracula, who is supposed to take the form of a bat and suck the blood of his victims. It's all nonsense, of course, but there are vampire bats.

The scientific name for a vampire bat is *Desmodus rotundus*, which means 'a bundle of round teeth'. Vampire bats are tiny beasties, and only grow to around 9cm at most. They do drink blood (of horses and cattle and – very rarely – humans), but they are harmless. In fact, their spit is very good for stopping blood clotting.

Is it a bird ... ?

No, it's a snake. Beware the parachuting paradise tree snake of Southeast Asia. It can spread out its skin and dart through the air for up to 45m, like some scarf scud missile!

Cloak and dagger

The black heron of Africa is a sinister little beastie. It brings its wings over its head like a dark cloak, waits until a fish enters the dark area and then grabs it with its sharp beak.

Blood-suckers

- Vampire birds – The tiny finch of the Galapagos Islands pecks at the backs of other birds until they bleed and then drinks their blood.
- Vampire fish – There are fish in the River Amazon that wriggle their way into your skin and suck on your blood. They are really tiny, growing less than 1cm long, and are transparent, too, so it's easy to miss them – until they latch on and start sucking …

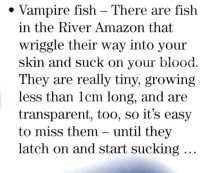

Deadly and hungry

Beware the black widow! It has a poisonous bite 14 times more dangerous than that of a rattlesnake and can kill within 48 hours.

The female black widow is not much of a wife. She eats her husband! She obviously likes men, though, because she can eat up to 25 husbands a day!

Bananas

The most poisonous spider in the world is the Brazilian huntsman, also called the banana spider. It has enough venom to kill six people.

Speedy spider

The African sun spider has great long legs and can scurry across the desert sands at over 16km/h – that's a bit faster than you can run. It runs this fast to get out of the Sun and can be seen scuttling from shadow to shadow.

For their size, these spiders have the biggest jaws of any creature. They have been known to cut hair for their nests. Fancy going to the hairdresser and having a spider cut your hair!

How many?

There are over 30,000 different types of spider living all over the world. In every square metre of countryside, there are about 500 spiders. In Britain alone, there are an estimated 500 trillion spiders.

Souper spiders

Spiders can't eat solid food. Instead, they paralyse their victim, inject it with a kind of liquid poison to turn it into a soup, then they suck it up like a drink. Yuck!

Silky steel

The silk spun by web spiders is 200 times finer than the finest human hair, yet it is stronger than steel of the same thickness.

Action spider

The tree-climbing tarantula of the West Indies is so fast that it can catch insects in mid-air. This huge, furry, red and brown spider leaps from tree to tree.

The real Superman of spiders is the Californian trapdoor spider. A trapdoor spider digs a burrow with a flap over it, just like a trapdoor, and then lies in wait, suddenly leaping out to pounce on its victim and drag it back into the hole under the trapdoor. The Californian trapdoor spider is immensely strong and can catch a victim 38 times its own weight. That would be like you catching two polar bears and dragging them both away at once.

Monster websites

The biggest spiders are hunting spiders, which live in holes in the ground. Web spiders are smaller but they can spin monster webs. The biggest webs are those of the long-legged golden silk spider and can be over 3m wide, like huge lace curtains. The webs are strong and can trap birds and even hinder humans.

GET THIS!

The biggest British spider is the Cardinal, which has a leg span of 12cm. It got its name because it was common at Hampton Court Palace in the 1500s and used to frighten Cardinal Wolsey who lived there at the time.

Hairiest giant

The biggest spider in the world could fit on your head like a cap! The Goliath bird-eating spider has a thick, bulbous body that grows around 9cm long, and great hairy legs that spread 28cm wide. The bird-eating spider keeps growing all through its life and can live for 25 years! Just think, there could be some really giant grandaddy Goliaths out there …

Although called a bird-eating spider, the Goliath rarely catches birds. But the pink-toed tarantula does. This is the Tarzan of tarantulas. It can leap from branch to branch and swim across lakes, and pounces on its victims.

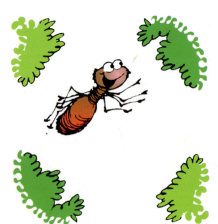

Sting in the tail

There are over 1,000 different types of scorpions. The biggest is the South African rock scorpion, which can grow up to 25cm long. The deadliest is the Tunisian fat-tailed scorpion of North Africa. One of its stings can kill a human in less than four hours.

Scorpions were amongst the very first creatures to live on land and have been around for over 440 million years, long before the dinosaurs. The biggest scorpion that ever lived was called *Brontoscorpio* and may have been nearly 1m long.

The whip scorpion can spray you with vinegar. Handy if you're eating a bag of chips.

Creepy crabs

Crabs can look a bit like spiders, with their long spindly legs. The crab with the longest legs is even called the giant spider crab. It has a leg span of over 5.5m, which means it could stand right over your car like a tent!

Giant spider crabs can weigh up to 18kg – that's nearly as much as four fully grown cats.

The giant spider crab would make a brilliant tap dancer, with all those legs. I wouldn't want to dance with it, though, because it can give a really nasty nip.

Biggest crab

The spider crab is the crab with the longest legs, but the crab with the largest body and claws is the Tasmanian giant crab. This crab can weigh over 16kg and has claws as big as human arms (just like Popeye's), each weighing 3kg or more.

Lobsters are even bigger than crabs. The biggest lobster ever caught weighed 20.14kg and was over 1m long.

Beefy-beetle

The heaviest insect in the world is the Goliath beetle. It weighs 90g, the same as two beefy sausages, and is heavier than 300 butterflies.

The Goliath beetle looks pretty frightening – well, both pretty and frightening, really. It grows up to 12cm in length and has long, spiny legs. It's also immensely strong. In fact, it's the strongest living thing in the whole world and can support 850 times its own weight. It can grip a branch so tightly, you would never be able to pull it off. If you were as strong, you could lift 38 tonnes.

The Goliath beetle is also quite beautiful. It's either black and white or a chocolate brown in colour, and is covered in a very light down, like fur, making it look a bit like a flattened tennis ball with legs.

Stickly and long

The rhino beetle isn't the longest insect. The Borneo stick insect is over 32cm long, and when its front legs are spread out, it's 50cm long! That's over twice the height of this book.

Rhino beetle

The Goliath beetle isn't the longest beetle. That award goes to the rhinoceros beetle, which grows 20cm long (the height of one of the pages of this book). Half of its length is made up of a pair of enormous horns with which it fights rival beetles. Battling males lock horns like two giant Viking wrestlers.

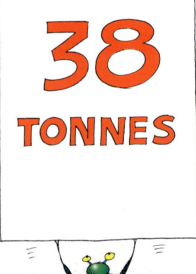

Biggest insect EVER

The biggest insect ever to have lived was a giant dragonfly called *Meganeura*, which lived 220 million years ago. Its wingspan was 70cm, and its body was 46cm long, nearly four times bigger than the biggest living dragonfly today. It must have whirred around the ancient swamps like a toy plane.

Biggest mini-beastie

You have to go to the Andaman Islands in the Indian Ocean to find the biggest living creepy-crawly. This is the giant centipede, *Scolopendra*, which grows 33cm long and 4cm wide. It's about the same size as a weasel (but with 100 legs!).

Depend-ant

The worker honeypot ant is force-fed water and nectar until its abdomen swells and swells and swells and becomes so huge that it serves as a larder for the other ants, which feed off it.

Chemical warfare

The bombardier beetle has a deadly dangerous fart! It has two separate chemicals stored in its body. When threatened, it mixes them together and ejects them from its bum. The poison comes out as a hot gas (around 100°C) at a speed of 12m a second.

Sticky feet

The Florida leaf beetle has feet packed with glue so that it can cling to leaves. The glue is so strong, it would be like you having a Land Rover glued to each foot!

Mega-creepy

The biggest creepy-crawly ever was *Arthropleura*, a massive millipede that lived 220 million years ago. It had only 90 legs but was 1.8m long, so it could fill your bed with feet.

Atom ant

Ants are normally tiny little things, but termite ants can grow quite big. The Queen termite is a huge bloated thing, up to 14cm long and 3.5cm wide (as big as a hamster!). She hardly moves but lays about 30,000 eggs a day and can live for 50 years.

Termites build monster homes. Their nests can be 6m high. That's like you and your mates building a skyscraper 8km high to live in! Over two million termites can live in one nest, and they've been building them like that for over 220 million years.

Wood you believe it

Termites are very greedy. It's possible to go to sleep at night in Africa and wake up to find everything wooden has been chomped into fragments – including your bed!

GET THIS!

King of poo castle

If one dung beetle tries to steal the poo ball of another dung beetle, then the rightful owner jumps on top of the ball and the other tries to knock him off!

Pooper-scooper

The dung beetle is an amazing creature that revels in eating poo! Some species collect dung into a ball and roll it home. They can push along balls of poo over 50 times their own weight at a speed of 0.8km/h.

Dung beetles can clear up piles of poo in rapid time. A 1.5kg pile of elephant poo was eaten or removed by 16,000 dung beetles in just two hours!

One species of South African dung beetle eats the poo left behind by a giant snail. In fact, the beetle rides around on the shell of the snail waiting for its next meal!

Eleph-ant

The driver ant of Africa is the largest ordinary ant, and can grow 3.3cm long.

The army ant of South America doesn't have a nest. Swarms of these ants march through the tropical forests like an army, devouring anything that gets in their way – even people if they don't watch out! There can be as many as 1.5 million ants in one army, in a column 10m wide and up to 800m long.

Ant-i-social

Robber ants raid the nests of other ants and then turn them into slaves.

The parasol ant builds its own garbage heap and lives off the fungus that grows there. Just think what it would do with your socks!

Body bugs

Did you know that there are loads of creepy beasties that can live on you, feeding off your blood or skin or other bits. Eergh ... I'm itching already!

Lousy lice

There are three types of louse that inhabit your body – the head louse, the body louse and the crab louse. They all have six legs and crab-like pincers so that they can cling to your hair. The female louse lays eggs at the roots of your hair. These eggs are called nits.

The crab louse, which lives on eyebrows, eyelashes, armpits or other hairy bits, spends its entire life clinging to just one hair. Body lice will crawl from one item of clothing to another, and head lice swap heads on a comb or a brush.

Blood sucking

Leeches also suck your blood and have long been used by doctors as a kind of cure-all. The biggest leech is found in the Amazon and grows up to 30cm long. A leech has three jaws (we have two) containing a total of 100 teeth! Smile please!

Worrying worms

The guinea worm gets into the body through untreated drinking water. It then finds its way under the skin where it dies. If any part of it stays in the body, it can cause a terrible fever. The dead worm has to be pulled out slowly through the skin so that it doesn't break. Some worms may be up to 1m long and it can take weeks to pull them out.

The hookworm is another revolting parasite. It bores its way into people through their feet and then works its way into the intestine where it fixes itself by hooks around its mouth. In tropical climates, one human may have as many as 500 million hookworms!

Gutsy worms

The tapeworm is a parasite that can live inside people's intestines. They can grow up to 15m long, or three times the length of the intestine. In fact, one has been found which was 23m long. This revolting worm could wrap round your waist 30 times!

Just a tick!

Ticks are revolting spidery-like things that attach themselves to your skin and feed on your blood. They can take in up to 600 times their bodyweight in blood. They glue themselves to your skin while feeding. If you try to pull them off, you could leave part of them behind!

GET THIS!

Your bed contains millions of dust mites. And each dust mite goes to the toilet constantly, leaving over 200 times its own body weight in poo during its short lifetime! Dust mites feed on our dead skin, so they don't actually bite us, but we can be allergic to their poo and that's bad if you have asthma.

Don't let the bed bugs bite!

Your bed may also be full of bed bugs. These bite and suck your blood at night. A bed bug can take 6 times its own weight in blood and spends up to 10 minutes feeding on you at a time.

Mini-monster

The most dangerous insect in the world is the mosquito. In fact, it's probably the most dangerous creature of all time. Around half the deaths of all humans who have ever lived have been from malaria inflicted by the malaria-carrying mosquito.

If a person strays into a mosquito swarm, he or she could be attacked by nearly 300 mosquitos every minute and they would suck out half of that person's blood in just a few hours.

Blood-suckers

The assassin bug has a large nose (called a proboscis), with which it stabs other insects and sucks out their juices. These bugs will attack humans and feed off their blood. One is called the kissing bug because it creeps on to your face when you're asleep and bites you.

The assassin bug loves bed bugs. So after the bed bug has fed on you, the assassin bug feeds on the bed bug!

Assassin bugs are usually found only in the warm tropical countries, but they are gradually heading north as the world's climate heats up!

GET THIS!

The praying mantis is a relative of the cockroach. After the male and female mantis have mated, the female eats the male unless the male is quick enough to dodge her huge jaws. The males are getting better at this and about two-thirds of them escape!

Immortal cockroach

The cockroach is a bizarre creature. It is almost immune to radiation, so it is the creature most likely to survive a nuclear attack. It can survive for up to a week even without its head. But don't let it near boric acid. It gets terrible wind and because a cockroach can't belch, its stomach swells up and explodes white pus everywhere!

Whopping wrigglies

What's the longest worm you've ever seen? Up to 10cms? 20cms? Well, beware of the boot-lace worm, which lives off the coast of Britain in the North Sea. It can grow up to 30m long, but the biggest ever known grew to an incredible 55m. That's longer than the longest-ever snake, and it could wrap itself around an average-sized house.

The giant earthworm of South Africa can grow up to 3.35m long and can stretch out to a frightening 6.4m. It could wrap itself round a car. Now I can't see a blackbird pulling that up for breakfast!

Maggot spit

Maggots can't chew food like you and me. They have to spit on it so that it dissolves and then suck it up like soup.

Monster glop

The biggest snail on land is the African giant snail. It can grow up to 39cm long and weigh up to 900g. That means it could stretch right the way across the open pages of this book – and just think of all that slime … .

Snail mucus is so thick that a snail can glide along the edge of a razor blade without being cut.

Most snails eat only plants but the Euglandina snail eats other snails. It stretches out its gloppy neck and mouth and clamps its jaws around its victim, tearing it up with its teeth.

Sluggish

The biggest slug is the great grey slug, which can grow up to 20cm long. It can stretch out to 11 times its normal length – or over 2m!

Some slugs can produce a cord of slime down which they hang till they reach the ground.

A slug lives about 18 months unless it's killed off by winter frosts. It lays about 25 eggs and if all these survived and they laid 25 eggs each and so on, then by the time the first slug died it would have had 18,000 descendants. One snail can produce 1 million descendants in 5 years.

---**GET THIS!**---

Slugs have tongues with 27,000 teeth.

Maggot remedy

Maggots may be revolting things but they can be helpful. Maggots of the bluebottle fly eat rotting flesh and, during the Second World War, they were used to help soldiers with severe burns by cleaning out their wounds.

Anyone for worm pie?

Here are some revolting things humans have done with creepy-crawlies …

- The gloppy eggs of the giant water bug are eaten as a delicacy in Mexico.
- Crushed ladybirds used to be put on infected teeth to ease the pain.
- The grub of the Goat Moth was a favourite food of the Ancient Romans.
- In Japan, you can eat worm pie.
- Some tribes along the Amazon River eat head lice and the bottom half of the giant ant – alive!
- The larvae of giant weevils are eaten in the West Indies.
- Native Australians love to eat the swollen witchety grub.
- Earwigs used to be crushed and mixed with hare's urine and then poured into the ears as a cure for deafness.

95

Index

a albatrosses 68
alligators 43
anteaters 26
antelopes 11
ants 86, 88–9, 95
assassin bugs 92

b baboons 25
bats 76
bears 30, 31
bed bugs 91, 92
beetles 84, 86, 88
Bigfoot 24
birds 68–75, 76, 77
boars and hogs 21,
23
buffalo 26

c camels 28
cats, big 10–11
centipedes 86
chameleons 41
cheetahs 11
chimpanzees 25
clams, giant 63
cockroaches 93
crabs 82, 83
crocodiles 42–3

d dogs and wolves 12,
13
dragonflies 85
dust mites 91

e eagles 69, 75
eels 63
eggs 62, 68, 72, 95
elephants 16–19,
43

f ferret 20
fish 56–60, 64–5, 77
flying foxes 76
frogs and toads 44,
45

g gibbons 24
giraffes 26, 29
gorillas 24

h hippos 22, 43
horses 27
hyenas 14

j jaguars 11
jellyfish 61

k kangaroos 15

l leeches 90
lice 90, 95
lions 10, 11
lizards 36–41
lobsters 82

m maggots 94, 95
mammoths 19
mongooses 46
moose 26
mosquitoes 92

o octopuses 62
okapis 26
orang–utans 24

p parasites 90–1
piranha fish 56
porcupines 21
praying mantis 92

pumas 11

r rats 20
rhinos 26

s salamanders 44, 45
scorpions 82
sea cucumbers 59
sea urchins 60, 61
seals 31, 53
sharks 54–5, 61
shrews 20
skunks 23
sloths 21
slugs and snails 94,
95
snakes 46–7, 76
spiders 80–2
sponges 64
squid, giant 52
stick insects 84
stonefish 60
swans 69, 72

t termites 88
ticks 91
tigers 10, 11
tortoises 34, 62
tuataras 40
turtles 34–5, 62

v vampires 76-7
vultures 70, 73

w walruses 31
whales 50–3
worms 90–1, 94, 95

z zebras 26